NURSERY RHYMES
FOR AN
IMPROVABLE WORLD

Graham Dukes

Liisa Helander drew the pictures

Order this book online at www.trafford.com
or email orders@trafford.com

Most Trafford titles are also available at major online book retailers.

Print information available on the last page.

ISBN: 978-1-4120-5752-3 (sc)

Because of the dynamic nature of the Internet, any web addresses or
links contained in this book may have changed since publication and
may no longer be valid. The views expressed in this work are solely those
of the author and do not necessarily reflect the views of the publisher,
and the publisher hereby disclaims any responsibility for them.

Any people depicted in stock imagery provided by Thinkstock are models,
and such images are being used for illustrative purposes only.
Certain stock imagery © Thinkstock.

Trafford rev. 05/29/2015

 www.trafford.com

North America & international
toll-free: 1 888 232 4444 (USA & Canada)
fax: 812 355 4082

for Amber, Julie and Maartje

CONTENTS

PROLOGUE

nce upon a very-long-time-ago, Nursery Rhymes had a habit of tiptoeing quietly and unobtrusively into the culture and staying there. Some, no doubt, were the progeny of poetically inclined nursemaids and whimsical uncles, and they were intended at first only for the family circle. Many others seem to have begun as comments (sometimes whispered in dark corners or smudgily printed as illegal pamphlets) on the events and scandals of the day. We do not as a rule know where they began, though with some dating back for seven centuries there are theories a-plenty. Did *Rock-a-Bye Baby* really start its life as a allegory on

King Charles the First of England, who hid in a Shropshire treetop from his Puritan pursuers? American historians have quite a different explanation of its origin. Certainly *Ring-a-ring-o'roses* was not at first a skipping game: it gives a passable account of the symptoms and signs of bubonic plague. And even if in some circles King Charles was considered to merit gentle ridicule, the plague did not. But both were the talk of their day, and when that day was past the Nursery Rhyme perpetuated it in popular memory, if only in the form of jingles more akin to doggerel than to poetry, though here and there with nicely archaic turns of phrase. Some were singable from beginning to end while others seem to have owed their attraction to a memorable line or two, thereafter letting us down with a bump:

One misty, moisty morning,
When cloudy was the weather,
There I met an old man,
Clothed all in leather,
With cap under his chin
How do you do, and how do you do,
And how do you do again?

The two first lines set a poetic scene in the yellows and browns of the autumn, but then it is as if inspiration runs out, or perhaps the small listener's patience could take no more and it was time for a mere rhythmic clapping game.

Whatever the true history of a particular rhyme, the fact is that, for several hundreds of years, such verses had a habit of slipping their moorings and sailing out into a bigger world - first by word of mouth and then in serious print - and once out there in that wide wild world they stayed, even after the world had found other topics to worry its head about. Perhaps there was not much to replace or augment the old rhymes. Old King Cole remained a Merry Old Soul; few would have thought it proper to celebrate Benjamin Franklin in a similar manner in his day, and though there was no shortage of eulogies on such worthy public figures these solemn poetic tributes hardly lent themselves to nursery reading. There were some misguided attempts in that direction:

When Sir Joshua Reynolds died,
  All nature was degraded;
  The king dropped a tear into the queen's ear,

And all his pictures faded.

Crowned heads were particularly sensitive to insufficiently respectful ditties. No-one, surely, would have dared to make light of Queen Victoria, who would in any case have declared herself unamused. Napoleon Bonaparte was made a figure of sarcastic humour at a safe distance across the English Channel, but the politics of the time were too much in evidence and the fun too tinged with bitterness for most of the rhymes to outlive their subject.

What did happen was that a very little of that century's lighter literature spilled over into the nursery. Edward Lear's *Owl and the Pussy Cat* made the grade and there it still sits comfortably alongside Little Bo-Beep in the anthologies, timeless as his *Yongie Bongie Bo*, and apparently safe for all eternity.

Just now and again in our time, verses on themes of the day have suddenly appeared among children, curiously anonymous, only to vanish again. Leo Meyler records a skipping rhyme which once went the rounds of Denver, Colorado and which in view of its subject could not have been older than the nineteen-forties:

Mother, mother, I am ill!
Call the doctor from over the hill!
In came the doctor, in came the nurse,
In came the lady with the alligator purse.
Penicillin, said the doctor
Penicillin, said the nurse
Penicillin said the lady with the alligator purse.

Almost at the same time, with the Nazi occupation of Western Europe, children in the Midlands of England were chanting:

It's raining, it's pouring
Hitler said to Goring
I've lost my pants in the middle of France
And I can't get them till morning.

But most such ephemera came and went, and the books of Nursery Rhymes looked the other way, still content to regale their readers with the merriness of King Cole and his fiddlers three or admonitions to an ancient Dame to get up and bake her pies. It is true that Eenie Meenie, Minie Mo did creep into respectable print for a while, but the notion of catching a nigger (or even in later versions an indian) by his toe raised accusations of racial indocrination and it was quietly discarded, except where the indian was in turn replaced by a tiger.

Perhaps, too, the colourful villains of yesteryear, genuine or fictitious, provided more inviting and less treacherous material for irreverent comment than do their successors in the twenty-first century. Nor did the villains seem very suitable: Tom, Tom, the Piper's Son, whose crime involved no more than the theft of a pig, still provided more digestible fare for the small stomach than did Sweeney Todd, Burke and Hare, or Dr Crippin, who were merely dark and lugubrious. As to matters of violence: it was simple and even a little thrilling to think of the Little Man who had a Little Gun and whose bullets were made of Lead, Lead, Lead; the Big Man with (real or supposed) Weapons of Mass Destruction is just amorphously gruesome. Guy Fawkes and his ambitious but flawed plan to blow up London's Houses of Parliament (and a great deal more besides) in 1605 with twenty five hundred barrels of gunpowder only made himself memorably laughable in the eyes of later generations:

Please to remember the Fifth of November
Gunpowder Treason and Plot…

One is hardly tempted to look back to the Ninth of September 2001 in quite the same spirit.

As to the professionals of our day: there have been plenty of poets whose lighter work could and should have twinkled in the nursery; Walter de la Mare in England, Annie Schmidt and Han G. Hoekstra in Holland, André Bjerke in Norway and many others have spoken delightfully, understandably and memorably for children in their time, but where the one has failed to surmount the language barrier the other has been too fenced in by copyrights and trade marks to find a lasting place in the broad world. Whilst we are about it, we must take a brief glimpse, in translation, at just a few of those delights from across the sea which we have missed for too long. There are so many others. No child in any language should be deprived of Annie Schmidt's thoroughly up-to-date mini-fairy tale in rhyme:

Over the waters of St. Kildare
There dwelt a damsel with nylon hair...

But for that, and for like missions across the

earth, we shall need an army of lyrical Translators with stars in their eyes.

And what else might we do now with our legacy of Nursery Rhymes? Whatever we do (or do not do), that legacy seems likely to romp unconcernedly into the new Millennium and beyond; nursemaids are already scarce and they may by the year 3005 not be around at all; but whoever manages the nursery (or the hatchery?) a thousand years from now is still likely to be raising with her charges the vexatious issue of London Bridge having fallen down and the need to build it up again.

In the meanwhile, those of us who were brought up in this tradition, with the old rhymes and phrases still echoing through our adult days, may like to ponder the question as to whether we might not apply them to saying something about today's earth - and tomorrow's. With their help we may find ourselves being critical, or amused, or perhaps merely rather more thoughtful about life as it races along around us. Is it so many miles to Babylon - in the deserts of Iraq - that we can afford to be indifferent as to what is going on there? In a world with ever scarcer resources, are we not a little too ready to live easily with disposables, wasting what we have left of the earth's riches? I may love little Pussy, but when it comes to the crunch how seriously do I take animal rights? Should we all not be poking a little (or a lot) more fun at bombastic commercialism before we become so immured in it - or brainwashed by it - that we no longer perceive its absurdity? And do we still have time to dream innocent dreams - or even sufficient peace of mind to sleep at all? The old rhymes in rather new jackets may just help us to see these things a little differently. Come, let us take a look.

Graham Dukes

ROCK-A-BYE BABY

Rock-a-bye baby
On the tree top
When the wind blows
The cradle shall rock;
If the bough breaks,
* the cradle will fall*
Is the world safe for a baby at all?
Rock-a-bye baby
Down on the lawn
Allergens, Pesticides, Salesmen and Porn;
If a wasp stings there'll be doctors to pay
And the porn and the allergens won't go
  away
Rock-a-bye babe
By the roadside instead
Decibels, litter, monoxide and lead;
If a car skids there'll be wailing and gore
And a blip on the infant mortality score
Rock-a-bye babe
To the sound of the seas
Sunburn and jellyfish,
  drain-borne disease;
If a shark rises there may well be cause
For a superhorrifical sequel to "Jaws"

Rock-a-bye baby
Safe in his cot?
Bedlice, tobacco smoke, gas leaks and rot;
And if there's no end to the rodents and fleas
Then it's out of the lodging and back to the
    trees

Rock-a-bye baby
On the tree top
No place is safe but this
    circus must stop;
The air is O.K., and the bough may be bent
But the chance of it breaking is zero per
    cent.

LITTLE TOMMY TUCKER

Little Tommy Tucker
Sings for his supper
What will he buy for it?
Cheese and a cuppa?
No, Tommy Tucker sits under the stars
Gorging on candy floss, Snickers and Mars
If he persists in these foolish adventures
Little Tommy Tucker
Will sing for his dentures.

AS I WAS GOING TO ST. IVES

As I was going to St. Ives
I met a man with seven wives
One for work, and one for play
And one to clear the mess away
Wife number four was cuisinière
And fed him true Parisian fare

Wife number five would darn his socks
As Mistress of the Needlebox
Wife number six was mainly seen
In pearls and silk and *crêpe de Chine*
And what that wife was up to… Fie!
Look at that twinkle in her eye!
(It seems that when men took a bath
She led them up the garden path)
But number seven contrived in fact
To keep the whole darn team intact;
Famed for her managerial skills
She ran recruitment, paid the bills
Appeased the Bank and checked the maids
For hygiene, honesty and AIDS
And after an exhausting day
She studied for an MBA.
Truly in life the biggest shots
Make good in some unlikely spots.

CURLILOCKS, CURLILOCKS, WILT THOU BE MINE?

Curlilocks, Curlilocks, wilt thou be mine?
Thou shalt not wash dishes
Nor yet feed the swine;
I am gifted and handsome, creative and rich
I can solder a solenoid, samba and stitch
I tolerate bloomers and girls who use bleach
Yet still I must plead and implore and
    beseech
Be callous or clumsy or clever - whatever -
So few are the things that I cannot condone
But never, please never
No, never turn up with a cellular phone

There once was a certain *panache* to a
    meeting;
White collars, a bow, a perfunctory greeting
And then in seclusion the ponderous forum
Would deal and debate in delightful
    decorum;
Lord, grant me such days as I cherished of
    yore
Ere the cellular chatterbox entered the door
Where it whistles and trumpets and jingles
    and jangles

While folk turn away at impossible angles,
To whisper and flirt and conspire and
   confide
In little alternative trysts on the side
And vital encounters they prize as their own
And scatter their banter and chatter world-
   wide
And occasion grey hair to the man in the
   Chair
Yet never say no to the cellular phone
I dwell amid cellular phones and survive
And still find some joy in remaining alive
But in intimate moments, in toilets, in trains
I cherish the fragment of peace that remains
Till when dealing with matters of moment
   in China
A squeaky Toccata from Bach in D Minor
Reminds me that tea with Aunt Joyce is at
   four
And can I drop in at the grocery store?
Curlilocks, Curlilocks, canst thou be mine?
Forswearing the ether, the chat and the line?
Abandoning such, though it cut to the bone?
And promise forever,
That never, no never,
You'll fall for the wiles of a cellular phone?

SING A SONG OF SIXPENCE

Sing a song of TV time
On Vegetarian Day:
Four and twenty blackbirds
Volunteer to play;
Hidden in a Lentil Tart
They get the cue to sing
And flutter round a banner reading
"Soya saved the King"
The King is on his carrot farm
Source of all his money
The Queen is eating sixpenceworth
Of sesame with honey
The Kitchenmaid, in lingerie,
Cries "Sexier with beans!"
Then hastily the blackbirds
Blank out the screens.

I TOOK THREE GRAINS OF MUSTARDSEED

I took three grains of mustardseed
And blew them into the air
To fly as the gathering dusk decreed
And I knew not whither or where;
With only a breeze to fondle and play
Only the trees to mark their way
The song of the seas as their roundelay
And only the moon above to care,
Only the moon to care…
One of my grains of mustardseed
Went as the warm winds blow
Thither where beckoning hedgerows lead
And gossiping brooklets flow;
Now blossoming mustard fields proclaim
Their joy, congealed to a rippling flame
Yet yield no murmur of whence they came
With only the moon above to know,
Only the moon to know…
One of my grains of mustardseed
Fell where the ages sleep
Where the mouldering tombstones give no
   heed
And the lovelorn ivies creep;
Where bud and green must wrestle alone

To glean such light as the elms condone
Then wither unseen among thankless stone
With only the moon above to weep,
Only the moon to weep...
But one of my grains of mustardseed
Bid me follow awhile
And I took the galloping gale as my steed
And the earth as my measured mile;
My home shall follow the tireless sun
And I shall roam as the torrents run
And comb the earth till my days are done
With only the moon above to smile,
Only the moon to smile...

THERE ARE FAIRIES AT THE BOTTOM OF MY GARDEN

There are fairies at the bottom of my garden
There are pedophiles parading through the
  land;
Am I fuddy-duddy formal if I feel they are
  abnormal
And the world is getting somewhat out of
  hand?

There are masochists in ecstacy in mantraps
There are fetishists in Fulham every day
And even cousin Julia is getting quite pecu-
  liar
And dressing up in father's old toupée

There are lesbians protesting on the Parkway
And sadists signing something in the Square
The odder folk around me neither stress me
  nor impress me
And it peeves them that I do not seem to
  care

There are fairies at the bottom of my garden
And buggers out with banners and a band

If I hurt them or divert them I shall say I beg
    your pardon
But I still admit I do not understand.

THREE BLIND MICE

Three visually disadvantaged mice
Sought counsel from an agro-engineer
Whose spouse had wrought a laser-powered
    device
To vitrify the lens and the cornea
Oh, thoughtless haste! They entered in
    reverse,
And, thence emerging, painlessly de-tailed
They sued; but since she proved no fault,
    - and worse,
Contributory negligence - they failed.

BAA, BAA BLACK SHEEP

Baa baa black sheep
Have you any wool?
Yes sir, Yes sir,
Three bags full
But wool's getting pricey and you ought to
   know
Where the profits and perks and percentages
   go

Three for my master, two for my dame,
Ten for the profiteer who lives down the lane
Eight for the shearer, two for his lads,
Twenty five percent for the prime time ads
Twenty for the wool mill
Spinning it with glee
Thirty for the middlemen…
Nothing left for me

Baa, baa black sheep
Would you keep your wool?
Yes sir, Yes sir,
Three bags full
The night's getting colder - and need I
   connive
To keep these rascals and rapscallions alive?

It's nylon for a nightgown, terylene for shirts,
Polythene for panties, taffeta for skirts
Rayon for a raincoat, satin for sarongs
And the sheepswool will stay where the sheep-
  swool belongs.

GRAHAM DUKES

IF ALL THE WORLD WERE APPLE PIE

If all the world were Apple Mac
The ocean IBM,
I would not cry Alas, Alack,
Though others might condemn
But firmly seeking my way
I would navigate, I think,
The Information Highway
And drive myself to drink.

I SPY, WITH MY LITTLE EYE

I spy, with my little eye
Something odd as my life goes by...

First I
Fall from the sky
Wriggle and cry.
And cry. And cry
Fie!
Sing, say the pundits, a lullaby

I,
Spry,
(Menarche nigh)
Flutter an eye
As the men go by
Start to long for a B.O.Y.
She, say the pundits, is none too shy

I
Spy
A suitable guy
Beta pi,
College tie,
Get all high
Shudder and sigh

My, oh my…
She, say the pundits, will multiply
I,
Poor I,
Misally,
As the years go by
I am deemed to supply
Parentage, porno and pumpkin pie,
Fritter and fry,
For ever and aye.
Gratify.
Satisfy.
I, say the pundits, must still comply
Try
Still to deny
That the good years fly,
But my skin goes dry
And I lose my taille;
So I buy
On the sly
Stuff to apply
(And beautify?)
Bienengelei,
Crême de Shanghai,
My age is a lie
Fools, say the pundits, falsify

I,
Old I,
Hors de bataille,
Think awry,
Spherify,
See the world with a jaundiced eye,
Creak and crumble and calcify,
Time, say the pundits, to say goodbye
Sigh,
Lie,
This time, die.
Putrify.
... Why?

THIS LITTLE PIG

This little pig smoked Malboro'
This little pig smoked Weed;
This little pig drank whisky
And this little pig used Speed;
But the wise little pig ate grass - and died
From the high residual pesticide.

LITTLE MISS MUFFET

The damsel Muffet, conscious of her duty
To cultivate a more than skin-deep beauty
Confined her fare to bran-embellished cakes
Washed down at times with low-fat yoghurt
    shakes
And, seated thus, upon a grassy knoll
Contained her lipids and cholesterol

A humble arthropod, no less inspired,
Seeking to be a purer, better spider,
Plucked up his courage; suitably attired
He landed on that grassy knoll beside her
Oh baseless fear, arachnophobic dread!
Shall friendship not be shared with generous
    grace?
The Muffet girl took up her tray and fled
Which shows that species thinking, far from
    dead
Thrives still among the whizz-kids of the
    race.

DING, DONG, BELL

Ding, dong, bell
Johnny's gone to Hell
Why did he go?
Someone ought to know!
Maybe he voted left, or right
Or smoked a reefer in the night
Yet these inconsequential things
Would merit neither hooves nor wings…
Bereft of virtue and of vice
Johnny, was neutral, normal, nice;
He did not pray, he did not sin
And nothing much went on within;
The Gods may fail to understand
Folk who are neutral, normal, bland.
The preacher's words did not enhance
His no doubt negligible chance
(Firmly discounted by his mates)
Of getting through the pearly gates;
Lost for a single thing to say
He merely murmured "Let us pray"
And bid us all in solemn voice
Advise the Lord upon his choice
Thus in effect, as you will note,
Putting the matter to the vote
For nor was Johnny qualified

For entry on the other side
And if he was not truly bad
The Devil might reject the lad
Unless he saw us handing in
Some testimonial of sin
And since there was no sin to tell…
How then did Johnny get to Hell?

It's better for our peace of mind
If Hell's recruiting Johnny's kind
We too have little hope of grace
*Perhaps there's **something** to the place…*

GRAHAM DUKES

HICKORY, DICKORY, DOCK

Hickory, Dickory Dock
The mouse ran up the clock
(Which shows that this trap
Is expensive crap)
Hickory, Dickory Dock.

ONE MISTY, MOISTY MORNING

One misty, moisty morning,
When cloudy was the weather,
I chanced to meet an old man
A-striding through the haze;
A fine man, a bold man
We tramped a while together
His every sinew scorning
His thirty thousand days
With time alone my master,
I can but think to follow
Though colours may grow dimmer
And riverbeds wax wide;
As ancient errors cluster
And certainties grow hollow
And recollections shimmer
Too faintly now for pride
But tramping in the bracken
Lies fortitude, to borrow
From splendid things that beckon
Upon that old man's course
My spirits reawaken
To thrill at my tomorrows
As new hopes drown the echos
Of wavering and remorse
When life's last shadows gather,

For minutes know no pardon,
I pray to suffer lightly
The parting of the ways;
Then, girded still and sprightly,
Shall clamber to my Father,
To lay aside the burden
Of thirty thousand days.

SIMPLE SIMON

Dr. Simon stopped a pieman
Going to the fair
Said Dr. Simon to the pieman
"Let me test your ware"
At that the pieman turned around
And he braced his mighty muscles
But Dr. Simon held his ground
And he flashed his badge from Brussels.
With mass spectrometry, scales and broth
He probed those marvellous pies
And noted his findings with mounting wrath
And a visage of pained surprise:
Four percent of them overweight,
A whiff of a humid cellar
Prohibited colorant fifty eight
And a dollop of Salmonella
The pieman plodded his homeward way
Bewildered and empty-handed;
A summons served for the fourth of May,
His retail trade disbanded;
While Dr Simon in virtuous zest
With the air of a righteous winner
Reported back on his noble quest
Then gobbled the pies for dinner.

LITTLE BO-BEEP

Little Bo-Beep
Has lost her sheep;
More prudent animal keepers
Can summon their flocks
From a little black box
By fitting the lot with bleepers.

GOOSEY, GOOSEY GANDER

Goosey Goosey Gander,
Where would you wander?
Chechnya? Liberia? Bosnia? Rwanda?
Whither will you wander
And what will Goosey find
To yet elude the slaughterhouse
With Michaelmas in mind?

Genocide in this place
Villainy in that
Hunger on the high ground
Flooding on the flat
Lechery in London
Graft in St. Tropez
Murderers in Moscow
Gaols in Mandalay
Robbers in Santander
Mafia in Rome
A Goosey, Goosey Gander
Can better stay at home

And when the farmer cometh
And bids you say your prayers
You take him by the left leg
And throw him down the stairs.

DR FOSTER

Doctor Foster, quack of Gloucester
Hypnotized three men
But the rest of the town
Soon bedded down
And never woke up again
Oh, the cost of a Doctor Foster
Master of untried theory
His ill-earned fees…
Excuse me please,
I'm feeling a trifle weary.

I LOVE LITTLE PUSSY

I love little pussy
She does me no harm
I have turned down a bid
From a furrier's farm
But the furrier's farm wants this medium
  grey;
They are raising their bids by a dollar a day
The furrier's farm is untruthful, at that;
They do not sell fur labelled "rabbit" or "cat"
They wash it and beat it, and later (I think)
It comes to the showroom as sable or mink

I love little pussy
I deprecate thugs
So I turned down a bid
From a maker of drugs
And creams and cosmetics, who somehow
  pretends
He is kind and humane to our animal
  friends
But the maker of drugs and cosmetics and
  creams
Has promised me riches transcending my
  dreams
His words are seductive, and should I give in

He will levy no fee for returning the skin

I love little pussy
Enough to ensure
That my marketing motives
Are worthy and pure
I shall weigh up the needs and the social
  aesthetics
Of furs and of drugs and of creams and
  cosmetics
Trade must not be hindered by one who demurs
On creams and cosmetics, on drugs or on furs
And once these fine folk have induced me to sell
Do you think I can trade little doggy as well?

JACK BE NIMBLE

Jack be nimble
Jack be quick
Take good hold of the candlestick
Brass is beauty
Brass is bold
Leaves the thanes of throwaway cold
Show them brass and they hold their noses
God provides and a fool disposes
Plastic ware, less quaint than queer
Wobbles its way through a brief career
Pales and perishes, presently passes -
Jack be valient - stick to your brasses!
Hold the fort till they turn the page
On the blow-away, tow-away throw-away
   age.

HEY, DIDDLE DIDDLE

Hey, diddle diddle,
Some sort of a fiddle
Has paid for our cow to fly
The brilliant thought
Of an astronaut
Intent on his milk supply
He has found too late
That the weightless state
And mould in the liquid air
Induces a flow
Not of milk or so
But of second-rate camembert.

GRAHAM DUKES

JACK AND JILL

Jack and Jill went up the hill
To fetch some heavy water
For Jack and Tom had built a bomb
(Jill said they didn't oughter)
But halfway there they met a pair
Who waved a flag with fervour
A Greenpeace man from North Japan
And a U.N.O. observer
The Greenpeace guy was a *samurai*
He urged compassion and calm;
He proposed a date to meditate
On a rural lotus farm
But - just to be clear - he added here
That disquiet ran deep and wide
Then he flipped with his sword, this feudal lord
Bowed stiffly, and stepped aside

It was U.N.'s turn to express concern
He spoke of a friendly mission
And the growing distress at Lake Success
With all this nuclear fission
But stressed as he might Jack's sovereign right
To desist, or not, or slightly
Then off he flew to the rendezvous
That the U.N. folk have nightly

36

See Jack and Jill ascend the hill
And they fill their bucket high,
They sing as they go of D20
But what of the *samurai*?
Oh, the Greenpeace lord did well with his
    sword
He has pierced the bucket's side
And the D20 flows out as they go
And is sprinkled far and wide
Then Jack falls down and breaks his crown
And Jill comes tumbling after
And somewhere on high a *samurai*
Is shaking with gentle laughter.

GRAHAM DUKES

HUMPTY DUMPTY

Humpty Dumpty sat on a wall
Humpty Dumpty had a great fall
All the King's horses and all the King's men
Couldn't put Humpty together again.

All the Queen's ladies and all the Queen's
  mares
Felt they must better this state of affairs;
There where the masculine chauvinist lingers
Trust to the cunning of feminine fingers!
Sewn up and knitted in pearl and in plain
Humpty Dumpty is seated again.

(The fact that his voice is little high-pitched
Has something to do with the way he was
  stitched)

HIGGLEDY PIGGLEDY, MY BLACK HEN

Higgledy, Piggledy, My Black Hen
She lays Eggs for Gentlemen;
Gentlemen come every day
Cajoling my Black Hen to lay,
While other fowl must needs cavort
With people of the meaner sort.

Her Eggs, to any reasoned mind,
Are undistinguished as to kind
Or taste or texture, yet they grew
To status symbols for the few
For which I gladly take the blame,
Author and agent of her fame;
Small wonder, as my vassals toil
Wrapping Her Eggs in golden foil
To tempt the most demanding eyes,
While other staff enhance supplies
(A euphemistic choice of words
Implying aid from lesser birds);
My advertising, most serene,
(Gracing "*The Tatler*" and "*The Queen* ")
Poetic rather than precise,
Flatters the fools who pay the price.

Higgledy Piggledy, see My Hen
Surrounded by these gawking men.
I smile benignly and extol
The stirrings of that kindred soul;
We both supply the world for gain
She serves the hungry, I the vain;
But as I cackle, strut and flirt
I grub more deeply in the dirt.

PEASE PUDDING

Pease pudding early
Pease pudding late
Full of salmonella on the sell-by date;
Most eat it early
Some eat it late
And get Delhi Belly on the sell-by date.

LITTLE POLLY FLINDERS

Little Polly Flinders
Sat among the cinders
Warming her pretty little toes;
Her mother came and caught her
And whipped her little daughter
For spoiling her nice, new clothes

Run, Polly run!
Sell the story to the *Sun*
"Sadism, mother and I!"
Cut some pretty deals
For the pictures of the wheals
And a shot of a shapely little thigh

Next for the Section
On Juvenile Protection
Foster Homes, Felony and Fault
But the matter of a Summons
And questions in the Commons
May mean that it isn't worth the salt

  Now jolly, with Polly,
And gaining from her folly,
Mother takes the TV stand
Declaring she has dressed her

GRAHAM DUKES

In Super Polly Ester
Fireproof Whiplash Brand.

FAIR, FAIR, MAIDEN IN WHITE AND RED

Fair, fair, Maiden, in white and red
- or should I be thinking of black instead?
No, youthful is youthful, and young I vow
To face the challenge of here and now
So sing with me, swing with me, loud and
   late
The night is velvet, the world is great
So dance to the drum and the tambouryne
For this evening, friends, I am thirty nine!
There's five more minutes to midnight's bell!
We'll rock 'em and shock 'em and give 'em
   hell!
Youth for eternity! *Vive la vie!*
For a thousand lovings is one plus me!
Three for partying, two for a bed
Or a bottle of bubbly will do instead
Manskin! Lambskin! Bless 'em all!
Twelve thousand nights until trumpet call!
Miss me? Kiss me! Get in line!
For four more minutes I'm thirty nine!

See forty creep through the gathering dusk
All joints creaking, a tang of musk
Courage, Comrades - I'm not afraid!

How dare he pounce on a youthful maid!
Let fifty rant and let sixty roar -
They won't get in, for I've locked the door
We'll let *them* mumble and freeze outside
In their middle-aged pique and their
    pompous pride
Fiddle-dee-dee for them - fetch the wine!
I'm still too busy with thirty nine!

When I am old, very old, like *that*
I shall take a voodoo into my flat
I shall dye my cat. I shall lead campaigns
For dope in churches and open drains
For monuments made to Mammon and
    Marx
And for public sex in the public parks;
I shall shake them stiff with the power of my
    pen
And dance them a ditty of virile men
And not for once shall I toe the line!
I've hardly started - I'm thirty nine!

One more minute til midnight rings
And shall I care what the morning brings?
X-bombs? Sex-bombs? Upturned toes?
Need for spectacles on my nose?
No, life is a torrent of love and right

And youth blooms still in a brave delight
So dance for the world and the grassroots
  grass
That we nurture to greenness as we pass
So here's to the night - do I hear the clock?
You expect me to tumble in shame and
  shock?
No, welcome tomorrow - for forty's fine -
It's even better than thirty nine!

MARY, MARY, QUITE CONTRARY

Mary, Mary, quite contrary,
Ecologically pure,
Tends her fields
And boosts her yields
With the finest farm manure
Mary, Mary spurns as scary
Chemicals, sprays and lime;
From sty and stall
She shovels it all
The muck of olden time
Sadly, my Mary reeks of the dairy
Could I now but contrive
To give her a scrub
In the laundry tub
And some Chanel Nr. 5.

CHRISTMAS IS COMING

Christmas is coming
The geese have gone on strike
Someone put a spanner in the postman's
  bike
Fir trees are moulting
The crackers getting damp
Santa Claus has syphilis
The Vicar got cramp
Power is uncertain
The Bank said no
The Cottage Cheese is turning
The Jag won't go
Family are downcast
The forecast too
If you're coming here for Christmas
God bless you

SIXPENCE, SIXPENCE IN MY SHOE

Sixpence, sixpence in my shoe
Round and silver, shining new,
Hand-held promise of a wonder
Dancing, I rejoiced aloud
Did not hear the distant thunder
For a sunbeam on a cloud
Mirrored all I thought to do
With that sixpence in my shoe

Sixpence, shilling, florin, crown
See a world that crumpled down,
Here a war and there a crisis
Crushed it in a cruel cascade
Days of gallivanting prices
Left me wondering and afraid
Limping through my life askew
Wanting sixpence in my shoe

Pound and dollar, euro, yen,
Guide me to the light again
Somehow, when the markets tumble,
Fortunes crumble, empires fall,
Take the rich but spare the humble
Poorer, let me yet recall

All the little dreams I knew
With a sixpence in my shoe

When the Angel takes my hand,
Leads me to the Golden Land,
May he bid the Lord forgive
Avarice and raw ambition
Vanities I thought to live,
But to smile on my contrition
For the tinier hopes that grew
From a sixpence in my shoe.

GRAHAM DUKES

WIDDECOMBE FAIR

Tom Peirce, Tom Peirce
Lend me your grey mare
All along down along out along lea
We want to confer out at Widdecombe Fair
With Caligula, Charlemagne,
King Herod, Ghengis Khan
Old Uncle Joe Stalin and all
Old Uncle Joe Stalin and all

How soon can strong men put the planet to
  rights?
All along down along out along lea
Perhaps in three days and a couple of nights
With Caligula, etc.

Well Friday was rainy but Saturday fair
All along down along out along lea
And Tom Peirce set out to retrieve his grey
  mare
From Caligula, , etc.

Disagreeing, alas, on a mutual course
All along down along out along lea
They'd partitioned the beast into packets of
  horse

For Caligula, etc.

Trust not the dictator who stoops to debate
All along down along out along lea
Remember the mare and her compromise
   fate
With Caligula, Charlemagne,
King Herod, Ghengis Khan
Old Uncle Joe Stalin and all
Old Uncle Joe Stalin and all.

PILLS FOR THE PURPLE PEP

There are people who I envy, they bewilder
and perplex
They're so blessedly superior in business,
sport or sex
Like Bill Gates or Cleopatra, Charlie
Chaplin and Tagore
And so many other persons whom we
cherish and adore
And I mutter, Man Alive,
What vivacity and drive
Full of energy and nerve
All initiative and verve
Full of gumption and of glee, all that is,
except for me…
So I called upon my neighbour and I told
her of my plight
And she said, I know the feeling, but the
tablets put me right
If you're teary or inferior you take one when
it starts
And she handed me a pillbox full of pretty
purple hearts…
Oh those pills with the purple pep, give me
pills with the purple pep

They are dynamite for damsels, they're the
flow without the ebb
I am scheming like a demon
I can face a thousand he-men
I can rocket through a wall
With no ill-effects at all
I can live a life of plenty as an impecunious
pleb
With my perfectly preposterous prescription
for the pep

I have novel sorts of notions which I scatter
here and there
Water closets for deposits by the sparrows in
the Square
For it all so unhygienic and unscenic what
they do
I shall offer them to Macy's now for ninety
cents a loo,
I have started on a letter
To *The Times* (or something better)
No, it hasn't got a theme
But it's vitriol and steam
I'm a serial explosion
Of creation and emotion
I took ninety-five subscriptions out to
Pravda in a week

That makes ninety-five calamities for all the
  other clique
Still my energy is bounding and resounding
  - what the hell
I took ninety-five subscriptions out to
  Glamour Girl as well
Oh, those pills with the purple pep, give me
  pills with the purple pep
They are dynamite for damsels, they're the
  flow without the ebb
I have sent a marriage advert
To His Grace the Duke of Bradford
Saying, May I be his missus?
And I filled it up with kisses
And if that is not sufficient bait to land him
  on the step
Then I'll take another purple heart to ginger
  up the pep.

Oh, the pep pill that is progress, that is
  nectar for a Queen
You should see what I embroidered here in
  ninety seconds clean
You're astounded by the quite unbounded
  energy I ooze?
It's a bonnet for a baby, but I've not decided
  whose.

Oh, those pills with the purple pep, give me
  pills with the purple pep
They are manna for the masses, they're the
  flow without the ebb
I am scheming like a demon
I can face a thousand he-men
I can rocket through the ceiling
With this effervescent feeling
I am urgent and resurgent - I am perfect,
  unsurpassed,
Let me take another - Mercy me - That must
  have been the last...

PAT-A-CAKE, PAT-A-CAKE

Privatize, privatize, baker's man
Bake me a cake as fast as you can
Bigger and richer and iced with a T
And a quantity discount only for me
Throw in the buns and some custard pies
What a splendid model of enterprise!
But if you're late you can tell your chums
You're out on your ear when the baker comes

Privatize, privatize, church from state
Cut-price bliss on a silver plate
Time for fun with the juicier sins
Before that paradise grind begins
Jazz up the Organ! Turn on the heat!
Shorter sermons! Compete! Compete!
For the church next door is beating the
   drum
For economy tariffs to Kingdom Come!
Privatize, privatize, order and law
Give me a judge I can bargain for
A lusty fellow with wit and pride
And a sneaking regard for my weaker side
I paid good money for board and keep
So judge me quickly and fine me cheap
And if those perks to the jury fail

I'll take a week in this fancy gaol

Privatize, privatize, Thatch and thrive
Where the poor give up and the rich survive
Where the weak die out and the strong
  succeed
Where charity pales before grab and greed
Where beauty withers and cash makes
  friends
Where certainty tumbles and fear ascends
And we shatter the structure of kindly care
In a grand eruption of *laissez faire*!

GRAHAM DUKES

THERE WAS AN OLD WOMAN

There was an old woman, who lived in a shoe
She had so many children, she didn't know
what to do

Which way would society tell her to go?
The prelates said yes, the abortionists no
The experts arrived at the shoe bearing
troops
Of condoms and tablets and spirals and
loops
And folders on knives and what foetuses feel
Which led her to ask for the floor and reveal

That whilst high fertility might have been
   causal
She now was unyieldingly post-menopausal
A pity, she mused, as they fought at her gate
She was just an old woman, regretting too
   late

Then she went to her husband
Who dwelt in the shed
Berated him soundly
And took him to bed.

THERE WAS A LITTLE GIRL

There was a little girl
Who seduced a belted Earl;
The curl in the middle of her forehead
Caused His Grace to believe
She was naughty but naïve
Though in fact she was artful and horrid
Like other wicked girls
Bent on sapphires and on pearls
Her income was out of proportion;
For however well she kept
Him smiling as he slept
She was even more adept at extortion.

I HAD A LITTLE NUT TREE

I had a little nut tree
Nothing would it bear
But a rotten apple and a worm-holed pear
Then rainstorms and brainstorms led me to
　a plan:
I dropped a silver dollar in the watering
　can…
See my little nut tree
All that it yields
American Express Cards, Access, Visa,
Shares in De Beers and the platinum fields,
Promissory Notes for the wealth of a Caesar,
Equities to shield me from drought-borne
　failure,
Junk Bonds to generate Gold Rush Fever,
Air-Miles to take me jaunting to Australia,
Letters of Credit on the Bank of Geneva…

Tomorrow the Fraud Squad will come and
　visit me
And all on account of my little nut tree.

GRAHAM DUKES

WHISPER, WHISPER, INTO THE WIND

Whisper, whisper, into the wind
Those dark memories best unspoken
Trust unhonoured and compacts broken
Unchaste notions that hurt and pain
Fancies uttered in hope of gain:
Hate begotten in spleen and spite
Scorn for those who stumbled or sinned
Cast such demons into the night
Whisper them, waft them, into the wind
Whisper into the midnight breeze
All the ills that defile creation
Artful ruses and obfuscation
Hunger stalking and crises steaming
Echoes of frightened children screaming
Time-bombs ticking their way to sorrow
Bleak hypocrisy, scandal, sleaze,
Things that must not blemish the morrow
Whisper them, cast them, into the breeze

Whisper, whisper, into the dew
Hopes for a day as the Lord intended
Tyrants tempered and fences mended
Murmur a promise to play thy part
With a patient hand and a sanguine heart

And tiny prayers, as the day arises
That God in his goodness may imbue
The day with a smile and some small
    surprises
Whisper them, scatter them, into the dew.

GRAHAM DUKES

SAM, SAM, THE DIRTY OLD MAN

Sam, Sam, the dirty old man,
Washed himself in the frying pan
Combed his hair with the leg of the chair
Sam, Sam, the dirty old man...

Sam, Sam, the wily old man
Marvelled how far his fame now ran
Sought the views of his Bank adviser
Sold his name to an advertiser
Posed with a pig for Coca Cola
Grunted praise for a deo-roller,
Played Sam's Song on a pianola
Sam, Sam, the wily old man

Sam, Sam, the wealthy old man
Filthier yet than when he began
Leered at the likes of the Drene Shampoo
   girl
Danced with the Princess You-know-who
   girl
Lauded gin like a true believer,
Sang about soap for Unilever
Caught the eye of the tax receiver
Sam, Sam, the wealthy old man

Sam, Sam, pathetic old man,
Ended his life as an also-ran,
Somehow his ads now lacked conviction
Sam well knew they were nine parts fiction
Once the spark goes, truth and pride show
Sam came clean on a Wash-with-Tide show
Got sold cheap to a travelling side-show
Sam, Sam, pathetic old man.

HOW MANY MILES TO BABYLON?

How many miles to Babylon?
Seventy score and ten
Can I get there by jumbo jet?
Yes, and back again
I shall not journey to Babylon
It may be humid or hot
There may be pain I cannot contain
And strife I would rather not
I want my image of Babylon
Formatted six by ten
Cut and stacked and sterile-packed
By the lady from CNN
Then even with crises and carnage
I can calmly sip my wine
For whatever is wrong in Babylon
There is soccer at ten past nine.

TOM, TOM, THE PIPER'S SON

Tom, Tom, the piper's son
Stole a pig and away he run
The pig was eat and Tom was beat
And Tom went howling down the street

Tom, Tom, moved with the times
Set his sights on more lucrative crimes
Burgled and rifled and knifed his way
Oh, what shall we do with the fellow today?
Speak of betterment, mercy, correction
Coddle him, coach him, reform him, guide
  him,
Teach him insight and introspection
Hire a psychologist to sit beside him
Pack him off to a young mens' college
Train him, aid him, preach and persuade
  him,
Clear his mind of unwholesome knowledge,
Send him home when you've quite remade
  him...

But just to be sure that we're safe and sound,
Lock up the piglets when Tom's around

THE NORTH WIND DOTH BLOW*

The North Wind doth blow
And we shall have snow
So where did the meteorologists go?
They ran down the sewers
To hide from the viewers
Who trusted their promise of Spring, heigh-
  ho
That a ridge of high pressure would bring,
  heigh-ho
With never a murmur of snow, oh no,
Never a murmur of snow

Occasional viewers
Who visit the sewers
Note crannies inside
Where the weathermen hide
The place is a meteorologist's dream
No weather to speak of and nothing extreme
A climate unchanged from December to
  June
And waters unswayed by the phase of the
  moon
And not a suggestion of snow, oh no,
Not a suggestion of snow.

*Dedicated to Mr Michael Fish, BBC meteorologist from 1972 to 2004, who never fell into such errors.

OLD MOTHER HUBBARD

Old Mother Hubbard, she lives in the lane
And a rose grows up to her window-pane
They saw her stumble, they heard her fall,
They found her weeping against the wall
Yet nobody waited to ask her why
(Did you hear the ambulance bell go by?)
For life is holy, but labels are holier:
This is a senile melancholia!
Calm her with tablets and easy patter.
*The tears of old women, they don't much
    matter...*

(So small is her world,
So simple her grief
So broken her spirit, beyond belief
For tired are her limbs and dim is the light
And she wanted to water her rose tonight...)

Old Mother Hubbard, they scrubbed her
    clean
And they stopped her weeping with Tranqui-
    lene.
They gave her an enema, clipped her hair,
They punctured her here and they pricked
    her there

Then they took their needles and drugged
  her flat
With pharmaco-this and pharmaco-that.
But where will an old soul find relief
For a broken heart, and bottomless grief?
A fig for the former, a pill for the latter.
*The tears of old women, they don't much
  matter...*

(They've taken her slippers and packed her
  rings
And gone is the feel of familiar things.
Hard are the bedsheets, harsh is the light
And who will water her rose tonight?)

Old Mother Hubbard is sinking fast
Time for a pharmaco-counterblast!
Call the Matron, in full regalia,
Old Mother Hubbard has renal failure!
Diet and dialyse! Never despair!
Ring the folks at Intensive Care!
Oh, sheer ingratitude - why oh why
Must Old Mother Hubbard now choose to
  die?
They gape in the ward, and sniffle and
  chatter

*The tears of old women, they don't much
   matter...*

(But did you catch what she tried to say
Or was it too faint, as she slipped away?.
Distant the voices, fading the light,
Will someone water her rose tonight?)

Old Mother Hubbard has had her day
May we all end up in the selfsame way!
Enema'd, Tranquilized, Sterile, Clean,
All wired up to some slick machine
But spared such trash as a broken heart
That won't show up on the progress chart
Here's to ulcers and ECG's
And the chemical trappings of real disease!
May the labs grow fat and the files grow
   fatter,
*The tears of old women, they don't much
   matter...*

(So Old Mother Hubbard has gone from the
   Lane
And yet the roots of her grief remain,
For age is misery, youth is right
And no-one will water her rose tonight).

DAFFY DOWN DILLY

Daffy down Dilly
Has flown back from town
Looks pretty silly
In stockings and gown
A day in the rain
And a night with the men
And you'll soon see this filly
In Levis again.

WHEN I SHALL LAY ME DOWN TO SLEEP

When I shall lay me down to sleep - so
  blighted
With sleeplessness - I can but toss and turn
And see, my pet neurosis has alighted
And views me from the corner with concern

At night my debts are larger, and the prices
More daunting than by day; I lie in dread
Of aches and pains and international crises
I count the pansies, papered round my bed

What thoughts are left to think? I ponder on
  it
Plumbing my mind, yet all in vain; suppose
I try reciting, something like a sonnet
Can I recall some Shelley? Here he goes:

O wild West Wind, thou breath of Autumn's
  being
If Winter comes can - something - *my sore
  need*
Ghosts - something, something - *An
  enchanter fleeing*
How does it go? And why did Percy bleed?

No-one to tell me; all the world reposes
The telephone stands mutely on the chest
My books are tired; my dictionary dozes
Mankind reclines, unhelpfully at rest
All children are asleep in their pyjamas
Each little bird sits drowsing in its tree
And in the Zoo, the walruses and llamas
Are all sleep, without a thought for me.
The owls are wide awake; I wonder whether
Some kindly owl might condescend to call?
But even then, could we converse together
Constructively, or yet converse at all?
Awake, so damned awake I am, and weary
Loose clouds like earth's decaying leaves are shed
Well, that was that. Shelley felt just as dreary.
Lord, how much longer must I stay in bed?

ONCE FOR A MOMENT, THE CLOCK STOOD STILL

Once for a moment, the clock stood still...
Yet only a child looked out at the night
And savoured the wonder of stardust falling
On misty pathways and dumb stone walling,
Phantom hues in the secret light
And shadows cast on a vine-clad hill
This was a moment that time mislaid,
And the darkness fondled it, cloistered it
   round
And cherished the pattern of thoughts
   unspoken
Threads of a dream that must not be broken
And in that darkness something was found
That was rousing, yet gentle, and unafraid
This was a moment from time concealed
When mystery beckoned and wonder came,
And with that coming bore trust in its
   wending
Rugged in tenderness, briefly unending,
Building a richness that has no name
Of secrets glimpsed in a realm revealed
This was a moment that time set by
For things which are timeless, and know no
   guilt,

Though the world spin madly and break
  asunder,
Rolling to doom in a peal of thunder
This is a wonder that shall not wilt,
And a moment that lives until time runs dry.

LITTLE BOY BLUE

Little Boy Blue, come blow on your horn
Pedestrian crossings are subjects for scorn
And ladies on bicycles matters for mirth
Five hundred horsepower proclaim your
  worth!
Let true men travel as true men may
On their ego trips down a hero's way
Bold and belted and puffed with pride
At beating the hell out of time and tide
Little Boy Blue, come step on the gas
Come sever your soul from the abject mass!
Impress yourself as the radials burn
Screaming in terror at every turn
Let true men travel as true men will
A hundred and seventy over the hill!
Revving and roaring in glorious greed
To a drunken crescendo of sound and speed
Little Boy Blue, how little you seem
Pelting along in your vacuous dream
And never a glance or a thought bestowed
On the tranquil wonders that line your road;
While plain men travel as plain men choose,
Pausing to chat and to patch their shoes,
You pass and vanish, as harebrains must
Down your lonely road in a swirl of dust

Where pomp grows hollow and pride
  despairs
For nobody sees you - and nobody cares

SEE-SAW, MARJORIE DAW

See-saw, Marjorie Daw
Johnny shall have a new master
He shall be paid
But a penny a day
Because he won't work any faster

See-saw, Marjorie Daw
Johnny is still with his master
Got to the age
Of the Minimum Wage
But a shilling a day spells disaster

See-saw, Marjorie Daw
Johnny's new master is failing
Gone to the wall
With his bankers and all
And the national economy's ailing

See-Saw, Marjorie Daw
Now we pay Johnny for lazing
The dole for his smokes
And his pizzas and cokes
And what it all costs is amazing

See-Saw, Marjorie Daw

These economics are crazy
A guinea a week
For the old and the weak
But what do we do with the lazy?

See-saw, Marjorie Daw
Johnny shall have a new master
He shall be paid
But a penny a day
Because he won't work any faster.

GRAHAM DUKES

I DO NOT LIKE THEE, DR FELL

I do not like thee, Mistress Claire
It is the fetid scent you bear
Of garlic on your hands and hair
I do not like thee, Mistress Claire

I do not like thee, Dr Fell,
The reason why, I know full well
It is that stale tobacco smell
I do not like thee, Dr Fell

This gruesome twosome, Fell and Claire
Might meet one day upon The Square
And, as with magnets, could attract
Each other in some pungent pact
But, as with magnets, Claire and Fell
Place pole to pole could yet repel
One therefore might suggest instead
A first encounter tail to head
If Fell should fall, then Claire might claw
Him, knees to bosom, on the floor;
Should they thereafter choose to turn…
No matter. That is their concern.

DIDDLE, DIDDLE DUMPLING, MY SON JOHN

Diddle, diddle dumpling, my son John
Went to bed with his headphones on;
But something with cymbals and Upper C
Caused high-tone deafness at twenty three
Turn up the volume a trifle more?
Delirium tremens at twenty four
While rappers and rockers and jazz and jive
Quite addled his thinking by twenty five
Daft as a dumpling, see my John
Laid out flat with his headphones on;
Twenty six, all pulp and jelly
And only a twitch of the upper belly
Betrays the beat as his entrails rock
Uncomprehending around the clock

DOCTOR, DOCTOR

She: Here on a street in the middle of time
Where the evening chills and the shadows
  climb
My spirit is faint as I worry and wait
And I knock once more at the doctor's
  gate…

He: I am your doctor, in bangles and braid
She: (Which fifty folk before me paid!)
He: And I face the fevers undismayed!
Heigh ho! Heigh ho!

She: Doctor, doctor, lend me your ear
For time is short and the crisis near
My heart is heavy, my purse is light
He: Then, madam I bid you a restful night
I'm a very fine fellow with savoir faire
She: Then, doctor, have you no second to
  care
He: Pray lady, do not stand and stare!
Heigh ho! Heigh ho!

She: Pray doctor, have you no cure for the
  pox?
He: Shall I come down when a pauper knocks?

She: Then if you have only a moment to
  lend
Pray touch my temple and comprehend
He: I'm a very fine fellow with lace on his vest
She: (And he tries to tell me that East is
  West)
He: Pray hold your tongue, for the Doc knows
  best
Heigh ho! Heigh ho!

She: Pray. Doctor, have you a pill for my
  head?
Of a word of compassion might do instead
But I will not, would not, could not plea
For a rich man's succour on bended knee
He: Your life is short, but my art is long
Pray do not interrupt my song!
Take up your mattress and run along!
Heigh ho! Heigh ho!

She: Doctor, doctor I only crave
Some of the care a Samaritan gave
He: Then come now, woman, and show me
  your tongue
For the hour is late and my song is sung
Good gracious!
Contagious!

GRAHAM DUKES

Pray madam, run as far as you can
For I am a clean and an upright man!
A very fine fellow in a gold sedan!
Heigh ho! Heigh ho!

*

He: I'm a very fine fellow, in rings and bows
She: Which is just as far as the splendour
goes
He: The way of the world is a mint for me
And all of my failures morts gueris!
A very fine fellow, in periwigged pride
She: And his carriage and coachmen wait
outside
Well, Lord forgive him, perhaps he tried…
He: Heigh ho! Heigh ho!

THE QUEEN OF HEARTS

The Queen of Hearts, she found some tarts
Cavorting in the hay,
The Knave of Hearts had hired those tarts
And promptly ran away
The hearty King
Had had his fling
And now, one may suppose,
Sought on the floor behind the door
His doublet and his hose.

The Queen of Hearts she liked those tarts
She nurtured them to flower,
And coached them in the various arts
Of party, pomp and power;
By fits and starts
They learnt, those tarts,
And scared the Kingly clique
With clarion call of "Votes for All!"
And *"Vive la Republique!"*

The Dame of Hearts has led her tarts
Beyond the age of queens;
She signs decrees on the threadbare knees
Of her presidential jeans
And the favourite hate

Of her erstwhile mate?
The puritanical laws,
Which people get from her *cabinette*
And her Parliament of Whores.

LITTLE JACK HORNER

Pity Jack Horner
Thrust in a corner
Far from the Christmas pie;
Thoughtful and dumb
He sucks on his thumb
As he wonders and wonders why.
Sometimes one knows why the outcast goes
He may be yellow or black
He may defect from a stricter sect
But what is there wrong with Jack?
Well, pomp and prejudice have their ways
They classify, group, and screen
So the simple and bland can understand -
And Jack is an in-between

Pity the lot of the in-betweens
Who are neither here nor there;
You fit the rule or you play the fool
And the bigots they scoff and stare;
And Jack must learn from tumble to turn
What bumbling bigotry means
Shall he take the bus for Them or for Us?
There is none for the in-betweens

So here is a toast to the in-betweens

GRAHAM DUKES

Neither whites, nor blacks nor yellows;
The one must choose for Arabs or Jews
The other for dames or fellows;
Half-and-half may be good for a laugh
But the anguish is now and near;
Let us eat to the guy with our Christmas Pie
Our Jack is a pioneer!

For bye and bye, when the Old Gods die,
We shall share the same aesthetics;
We shall all be made in a khaki shade
A product of mass genetics;
And standing proud in the global crowd
Enriched by a thousand genes
We shall set the pace for a beautiful race -
We shall all be in-betweens.

JACK SPRATT

Jack Spratt could eat no fat
His wife could eat no lean
And so they built, the two of them,
A healthy food machine
A mixer and a centrifuge, a filter and a spout
And something flat, deprived of fat and
    freed of lean, came out;
For hours the Automat devoured
An epicure's delight
From venison to vitamins, from stroganoff
    to Sprite
From gherkins through to glutamate,
From Feta cheese to figs
The front side oozed their frugal goo, the
    rear supplied the pigs

Jack Spratt grew oddly fat
His wife began to waste,
They laced their goo with fibre stew
And aspartam to taste
With little use, their teeth grew loose
Their heads grew topsy-turvey
With peeling arms and itchy palms
Till the doctors warned of scurvy;
Yet every week with many a shriek,

With whistle and whirr and whine
The Automat gleaned lean and fat and cast it
    to the swine.

Jack Spratt is faint and flat
How weak his lady stands!
The doctor sighs, takes up his hat,
Retires to rinse his hands
And there beholds the Automat
He hears it grate and grunt;
A pause; then, with no heed for that
He turns it back to front

The couple Spratt with their Automat
Are gurus in nutrition
Folk visit their flat to experience that
And examine their fine condition
To see the device both scrape and slice
And rattle and grind and strain
And they taste the goo as it oozes through
Now why do the pigs complain?

GEORGIE PORGIE, PUDDING AND PIE

Georgie Porgie, pudding and pie
Kissed the girls and made them cry
Scurf and acne, stubble and scratch
Made for a most unwholesome match
But what of Clearasil, deo, Gillette,
Is there no hope for Georgie yet?
Hardly a hope, though the times have
  moved
Georgie is altered, but not improved;
Pink and smooth with his scented locks
He kisses the girls and gives them pox.

LEO IS ILL

Try to talk softly
Be still for a while,
For Leo, the boy with the great big smile
Who's clever and tall
And as strong as us all
Leo is ill

I went to see Leo this morning
His Mum took me into the house
She said, "You've come round for Leo, I see
Just follow me
But quiet as a mouse…"

Leo just lay there, ever so white
He looked so tiny, it didn't seem right
In his pyjamas, tucked up in bed
So I said to Leo, "Well, get better quick"
And he said: "Yes Dick".
I could hardly tell what he said.
And on his table, to make him well
Were bottles of stuff with a nasty smell.
It was sunny outside,
And the hurdy gurdy played on the hill,
But all I could think of was:
Leo
Leo is ill.

SHORT-SIGHTED

Speak not to me of glasses - I abhor them
My world is one composed of blobs and
    smudges
The blobs stand still, I know them, or ignore
    them
But all those moving smudges one misjudges

A nincompoop they call me, and a nit;
My oculist, my friends and my relations
Wear spectacles, but do not have the wit
To muse on my myopic compensations
I see the rose - I seldom see the louse
Floors have no splinters - and I shall not
    ponder
Upon the unseen litter in your house;
My world is small and smug; the rest is
    yonder.
Trams bother me; I catch the number three
Instead of number nine. And, yes, I tumble
Down stairs which I have not contrived to
    see
But misty life is sweet - I shall not grumble

For only I will see that kangaroo

With young and all, bounding across the
  square
Quite charming. Though I subsequently do
Confess he could not truly have been there.
So I go on, I blunder, I bewilder.
Look, Father Brown! (Or is it Aunt
  Matilda?)

SOLOMON GRUNDY

Genius Grundy
Recognized Sunday
Cloned on a Monday
Two and then four and then eight of him
　Tuesday
Dozens and hundreds and hordes of him
　Wednesday
Overran Harvard and Microsoft Thursday
Up to a voting majority Friday
Senator, Governor, President Saturday
Vetoed the cloning of other folk Sunday
Such are the lives of Genius Grundy

GRAHAM DUKES

BAT, BAT, COME UNDER MY HAT

Bat, Bat, come under my hat
Duck, swim in from the weather
Hen, hen, be safe in my den
And let us be jolly together

May every Tate have a Lyle for his mate
Each Pussy Cat find her Owl
May the Scrooges and Marleys celebrate
Togetherness, cheek by jowl

So ape, ape, warm up in my cape
Marks, come into my Spencer
Goat Goat, come under my coat
(Line deleted by censor)

MARY HAD A LITTLE LAMB

Mary had a little lamb
She fed the beast on strawberry jam
And when the creature met its fate
Upon some epicurean plate
The gourmets hailed *Agneau aux fruits*
Du Chateau de la Belle-Marie.

HOT CROSS BUNS

Hot Cross Buns
Hot Cross Buns
One a penny, two a penny
Hot Cross Buns
Empty are our purses
And still the money runs
One a dollar, two a dollar,
Hot Cross Buns.

Cheap, Quick, Loan!
Cheap, Quick Loan!
Easy credit, sleazy credit
Cheap Quick Loan!
Staving off the bailiff
By picking up the phone
Easy credit, sleazy credit
Cheap Quick Loan!

Bad, sad debt
Bad, sad debt
Dangle hope, strangle hope
Bad sad debt
Hurry to your father
Who's not insolvent yet
Dangle hope, strangle hope

Bad, sad debt.

All gone bust
All gone bust
Visciously, suspiciously
All gone bust
Nation in inflation
And no-one left to trust
Spare a nickel? Share a nickel?
All gone bust...

MONDAY'S CHILD IS FAIR OF FACE

Monday's child was fair of face
And she had no need of schminking
Yet folk who lauded her virginal grace
Knew never what she was thinking…

Forwarned that vanity led to vice
That ostentation would claim its price
That chastity called for a sacrifice
On the Puritan path to a Paradise
Where perfumes and paints were banished…

Yet still she cherished what some would
   deem
A futile folly, a covert dream
She digested advertisements by the ream
Believing such things are what they seem
And mused upon Helena Rubenstein
And beauty parlours with perfumed steam
Then she emptied her purse to the last
   centime
Betook herself to a store agleam
With powders and potions and paints
   supreme
For decking her dermis with self-esteem

Then she hid herself by a silvery stream
And smeared herself with vanishing cream -

... and vanished.

ONE THOUSAND AND ONE

When the year one thousand and one was
  born
It dawned with a bleak surprise
For no millennium hailed the morn
With trumpets rending the skies;
In the year one thousand and one, the earth
Was empty and cold and grey;
And famine and pain struck time and again
And the Time of the Dark held sway.
But the land of promise was not yet nigh
The day was windy and raw
So the ploughman turned away with a sigh
To plough a millennium more…

In need he ploughed as he prayed aloud
In faith he furrowed the land;
But famine and fear fell hard on the year
And dogma guided the hand;
And even as pestilence had its day
And some were succoured and fed,
So the perils of plenty came their way
And avarice ruled instead;
And though the world grew a trifle wise
And as old ills came to tire,

So hands now freed grasped out in their
  greed
And hope gave way to desire...

We have known the scars of a myriad wars
As the plough has bowed to the blade
We have wept the tears of a thousand years
Till the dreams of blessedness fade;
We have soured the rain and hitched our
  train
To gold and to hard travail
Yet should we follow that creed in vain
Shall faith and fortitude fail?
Or can man strive with a kindlier mind
And a will that is firmer and free
For that promised land - shall we understand
By the year three thousand and three?

A MAN OF WORDS

A man of words but not of deeds
Is what the Peace of Nations needs
A harmless case of logorrhoea
Who never thinks to interfere
Yet speaks in platitudes of pride
And leaves us feeling warm inside;
Ours not to comprehend his lore
But let us vote him in once more.
A man of deeds but not of words
Can tame the torrents, pluck the birds
Conjure with gigabytes or gold
While fierce orations leave him cold;
His not to argue or refute
The more they talk, the less they shoot
But he it is who fills the moat
To keep the ship of state afloat
A man of words and deeds bereft
Born neither eloquent nor deft
Who senses neither lust nor need
To raise the rabble, shoe the steed,
To scrub or screw, To rant or rave
Contended soul! Let others slave
That mardling mortals, such as I
May sit and contemplate the sky.

AS I WALKED BY MYSELF

As I walked by myself
I talked by myself
And myself said unto me:
Secure thyself and immure thy self
And pay what it takes to insure thyself
Or nobody cares for thee, no,
Nobody cares for thee
So I up and ran
To the Sun-Life man
And the kindly folk from the Pru
Whose crocodile tears redoubled my fears
Of plagues and scourges throughout the
   years
And frightening fates in view, oh,
Frightening fates in view
They told me of folk
Who choked on a Coke
Or met an uncharted doom
Some seized by a horde at a lonely fjord
Some mauled by monsters while uninsured
And borne to a pauper's tomb, yea,
Borne to a pauper's tomb

Now I starve with zest
At the Pru's behest

To be covered from A to Zee
As I pay vast premiums by the rules
Attuned to the risks of collapsing stools
And dark encounters with ghosts and ghouls
With bucking broncos and biting mules
With thieving trollops in vestibules
Or reckless rascals from driving schools
And prowling piranhas in bathing pools -
And sadly I gaze on incautious fools
Susceptible as they be
Then I walk by myself
And talk by myself
Since little else left is free
But a crust of bread tastes better than *bisque*
With underwriters to cover my risk
And my premiums care for me, oh,
My premiums care for me.

IF YOU WERE KING OF PICARDY

If you were king of Picardy
And I were Pope of Rome
We'd stride in circumstance and pomp
Under some gilded dome
And thrill to hymn and heirogram
Till time should pass us by
But I was boy in Birmingham
And you a lad from Lye

A life ago, my Birmingham
Was grime and smoke and haze
Where humble folk, unblessed by fame
Pursued their various ways
Yet style there was, and pride aflame
Under that sullied sky
When I was boy in Birmingham
And you a lad from Lye

The yellow tram of Birmingham
In tall unhurried pride
With oak and brass and frosted glass
Gonged lesser things aside
Stern hands would wield its rheostat
With harrowing points to ply
A gilded dome for me was that

111

And you, a lad from Lye

They took my tramcar, torched its track
They tore its walls apart
Reduced its frame to soulless scrap
Burnt through its ponderous heart
Thus snorting bus and urgent van
Condemned my tram to die
While I was far from Birmingham
And you a world from Lye

Under some sad and fateful star
Fell silence round the gong
And calls to "Pass along the Car!"
The Car had passed along;
Yet when I dream, I hear my tram
Still rumbling nobly by
Then I am boy in Birmingham
And you a lad from Lye.

THERE IS A LADY, SWEET AND KIND

There is a lady, sweet and kind
Whose every word doth please my mind
Though distant beam her radiance yet
She surfeth on the Internet
Dear soul: Whereto? Wherefore? Where-
 from?
Why veiled so chaste @compu.com?
I durst not ask, nor comprehend
That which thy fervent hand hath penned
Where whimsies wild alight with ease
To sparkle in parentheses
Flinch not, kind soul, though pedants start
Fleet is thy hand, untamed thy art
No doubts impede, no stops defile
The flow tempestuous of thy style
Thy hyphens glow, thy fancies fly
And I shall love thee till I die
Ere virtual bricks and graphic clay
Crash down, and lust and life decay
Ethereal creature, see my hand
Embrace thy fleeting ampersand
My moon, my mouse, my e-mailette -
Dark Lady of the Internet!

THE HOUSE THAT JACK BUILT

This is the house that Jack built -
Here, where once bright rivulets ran
And satyrs tripped to the pipes of Pan
Here in a maze of trouble and tears
In the merciless grind of a hundred years
This is the House that Jack built…
This is the Earth, all tattered and torn
Here are the oceans, all forlorn
Here are heartlessness, pride and scorn
Here are the poor, all worried and worn
The leafless tree and the fruitless thorn
Here, where the smokestacks spew and
   spawn
The brimstone rain to blacken the corn
And still the plans are cunningly drawn
To quicken the pace
To hover in space
To further the chase
And better the race
Yet here is a cow with a crumpled horn
And here is a child with a mindless gaze
Condemned in emptiness all its days
To live in the House that Jack built
And there is Jack, all debonair,
All I-don't suffer-so-I-don't-care

Who chased the dollars to fire the greed
That fanned the flames of imagined need
That robbed the oceans and scorned the
  chaste
That riled the frugal and piled the waste
That sullied the breezes
That blew in vain
To scatter the sleaze
That blackened the rain
That bared the forest and raped the corn
Begat the cow with the crumpled horn
And echoed creation's work defiled
In the vacant stare of a mindless child
And this is the house that Jack built?

GRAHAM DUKES

ACKNOWLEDGEMENTS

There are many anthologies of the Nursery
Rhymes of the English-speaking world. The
oldest known is "Tom Thumb's Song Book, "
published in London in 1744. The classic collection is the "Mother Goose Nursery Rhymes"
which appeared in 1780, with enlarged editions
to follow. Large numbers of Nursery Rhymes,
not all of which deserve the name, have been
collected on various internet sites, some citing
as many as five hundred verses.

The great bulk of the verses in this present
volume have taken their inspiration from these
classic sources, a fragment of the original text
usually being retained in italics in the opening
lines.

The present versions of "I spy, with my
little eye", "Doctor, Doctor", "One thousand
and one" and "Old Mother Hubbard" were
originally written in slightly different form by
the present author for the Regional Office for
Europe of the World Health Organization.

Four of the verses in this collection are free
translations and adaptations of verses originally published in Dutch by authors from The
Netherlands between 1945 and 2000. "Leo is

ill" is based on *Leo is ziek* by Han G. Hoekstra (1906-1988); "Pills for the Purple Pep" is liberally adapted from *Oh! Zo'n pilletje voor de pep*, a lyric composed by Guus Vleugel (1932-1998) for the Lurelei Cabaret, Amsterdam. "Short-sighted" and "When I shall lay me down to sleep" are free adaptations and translations of the poems *Bijziende* and *Vier uur 'smorgens,* both by Annie M.G. Schmidt (1911-1995). The fragmentary quotations italicized in the latter verse are from *Ode to the West Wind* by Percy Bysshe Shelley (1792-1822), who is unlikely to be upset.

Printed in the United States
By Bookmasters